MW00641602

Contents

PHANTOM RANCH

GRAND CANYON NATIONAL PARK

SCOTT THYBONY

ACKNOWLEDGMENTS

Certain individuals generously shared their time and enthusiasm during this project. Special thanks go to Ron Clayton, Pam Cox, Sjors Horstman, and Warren Tracy. Michael Quinn and Sara Stebbins pointed me toward useful sources, including material by Teri Cleeland and Keith Green. Muchas Gracias! — S.T.

Grand Canyon Association

Grand Canyon Association is a nonprofit organization whose mission is to cultivate knowledge, discovery, and stewardship for the benefit of Grand Canyon National Park and its visitors. Proceeds from the sale of this book will be used to support the educational goals of Grand Canyon National Park.

Printed in the United States of America

Project Manager: Faith Marcovecchio

Editorial: L. Greer Price and Faith Marcovecchio

Cover Design: Ron Short

Book Design: Ron Short and Larry Lindahl

Photographs:

S & A Partners, Sherri Curtis and Alfredo Conde: front cover, pages iv, 5, 6, 8, 10, 11, 12, 13, 14.

Larry Lindahl: pages 1, 2, 3, 4, 7, 9, 15, 16, 21 bottom, 25, 26, 27, 28, 29, 30, back cover.

Grand Canyon National Park Museum Collection: inside front cover (GRCA 4970), iii (GRCA 31401), 17 (GRCA 17656), 18 (GRCA 10091), 19 top (GRCA 4453), 21 top (GRCA 16951), 22 bottom (GRCA 7086), 23 (GRCA 10105), 24 (GRCA 10117).

Kolb Collection, Cline Library, Northern Arizona University: pages 19 bottom (NAU.PH. 568-789), 20 (NAU.PH. 568-323), 22 top (NAU.PH. 568-4684).

Map: Kevin Kibsey

Introduction

A SINGLE FACT SETS PHANTOM Ranch apart from anywhere else on Earth. It lies deep in the Grand Canyon, lost in a vast expanse of cliffs and gorges. To understand Phantom Ranch, you have to come to terms with the immense scale of its setting.

When the first Spanish explorers arrived at the rim in 1540, they saw the river deep below and estimated it was only six feet wide. Three of their best climbers scrambled down to investigate and returned exhausted after a long day of it. They got only part way down, but far enough to realize they had seriously underestimated the width of the river. And rocks they thought were the size of a man when seen from above were actually taller than the 185-foot tower of Seville.

Phantom Ranch covers only fourteen acres within a national park extending for almost 2,000 square miles. A dot on the map would exaggerate its size. But a trip to the ranch puts the canyon into perspective. It takes days by river, hours in the saddle, or long miles on foot. If you use the Bright Angel Trail, as most do, you find yourself following the trace of a massive fault that extends across the gorge, opening springs and breaching cliffs to create a natural cross-canyon corridor. The trail begins by dropping into a colossal amphitheater, a great bite taken from the flank of the canyon, which is a mile deep if you could fold back your wings and dive straight down, but eight miles by trail. As you descend, solitary buttes rise above

left: Looking up Bright Angel Canyon from the South Rim.

1

hidden canyons, and the distant rim overshadows an expanse of sunken plateaus and sky islands.

On foot you study the hikers coming up, for clues to what lies ahead, and learn the future will be sun burnt and soaked in sweat. Odds and ends of gear—warm clothing, bulky sleeping bags, even lanterns—lie next to the trail, temporarily jettisoned by uphill trekkers. On muleback you find the scene framed by two long ears as you descend the cliffs tier by tier. At each switchback the mule heads toward the cliff edge as if it intends to keep going. And then with perfect timing it turns at the last possible moment. "But don't worry," one wrangler said. "If you're afraid of heights just close your eyes—that's what the mules do."

Boat Beach on the Colorado River near the Kaibab Suspension Bridge.

Near Indian Garden the grade eases and a ribbon of green appears along Garden Creek. But soon the trail resumes its downward tilt, losing elevation and gaining heat as it goes. You notice the trees fading away as the desert takes hold, all skin and bones now with a scatter of plants—stiff, prickly, and spiked. Going to Phantom Ranch, you descend a stairway of life

zones revealing a microcosm of western North America. Stands of conifers are only a memory by the time you enter the mesquite-dotted landscape far below.

Pounded into dust by hoof and boot, the trail descends the Devils Corkscrew into the V-cut of the Inner Gorge. Cliffs of bare rock throw off waves of heat tossed back by facing cliffs. The day hardens under the full sunlight. Nothing moves except the swing of feet or the rocking gait of your mule until you reach the Colorado River where the current riffles and twists along the floor of the canyon.

Now you follow a trail blasted from the high cliffs of the gorge. And after trudging through sand pockets, you cross the Bright Angel Suspension Bridge on foot or continue along the River Trail to the mule-friendly Kaibab Suspension Bridge. These are the only dry crossings between Marble Canyon and Lake Mead, a distance of over 300 miles by road. You soon reach Bright Angel Creek where cottonwoods, arrowweed, tamarisk, and willow crowd the streamside in a burst of green. Hikers slump in the shade doctoring blisters or sit chin deep in the swimming holes, waiting for the creek to revive them. Each fall, rangers break out the handmade dams to allow the flannel-mouth suckers, brown trout, and rainbow trout to swim upstream. The trail continues past the ranger station to a line of cabins curving with the natural bend of the canyon wall.

Pools of shade collect beneath the cottonwood and sycamore trees, and the hypnotic sound of flowing water carries on the still air. Packs fall to the ground with a thud; riders stiffly dismount. You have reached the only place below the rim where you can take a shower, find ice, or sleep in a bed with clean sheets. A canyon oasis.

For some it's the perfect hideaway, and for others a gateway to even more remote corners of the canyon. In 1922 Mary Colter named it Phantom Ranch.

Phantoms and Bright Angels

As an architect for the Santa Fe Railroad, Mary Colter designed the new lodge to blend with the dramatic natural setting. She also searched for the right name to evoke the mood of the place. Thankfully, she discarded the initial choice, "Roosevelt's Chalet," and took the name from nearby Phantom

Phantom Ranch cabins, scattered among the cottonwoods on the canyon floor.

Creek, which flows from a deep narrows a mile above the ranch. The name of the creek came from the tributary canyon it drains, but the mystery lies in how the canyon got its name.

At least a dozen stories have circulated about its origin. An early newspaper account claimed the name came from a veiled figure who became visible at night on the canyon wall. Many had seen it, the reporter stated, but unfortunately he wasn't one of them. Others claim it came from the ghostly streaks of white calcite deposited high on a nearby cliff. One story, dating to the 1930s, says First Man emerged from the underworld in the upper reaches of Phantom Canyon. In the spring of the year, the legend goes, ancestral spirits return there in the form of black butterflies.

But the most probable account comes from Colter herself. The early surveyors, she said, noticed how the gorge kept disappearing in the afternoon haze, making it difficult for them to map. Crews working under François Matthes in 1902 did much of their mapping from the canyon rims using only a plane table and alidade. When they tried plotting the twists and turns of the distant cleft, the contour lines kept overlapping and, on paper, the canyon vanished.

The naming of Bright Angel Creek is more straightforward, since John Wesley Powell wrote a firsthand account of its discovery. But he took certain liberties in the retelling. In 1869 Powell and his men descended the Colorado River through the virtually unknown Grand Canyon.

Ranger's cabin above Bright Angel Creek.

The first boatman to reach the clear-flowing stream gave a shout, glad to find good water after days on the silt-charged river.

Powell originally named it Silver Creek, but by the time he published an account of his adventures many years later, the name had changed. They had already called a muddy stream found upriver the Dirty Devil River, so to balance the equation Powell named this one the Bright Angel. "The little affluent which we have discovered here," he wrote, "is a clear, beautiful creek, or river, as it would be termed in this western country, where streams are not abundant."

Phantom Ranch is nestled at the bottom of the Inner Gorge.

Weathered cliffs hang in a state of suspended collapse where masses of black schist and red granite push upward. And everywhere twist the dry washes and the side canyons, named and unnamed, branching toward the rims.

Bright Angel delta, cobbled with boulders washed down from every layer of the canyon, spreads out below. Here creek flows into river, branch canyon meets trunk, and trails connect. Half a mile up Bright Angel Canyon, Phantom Ranch lies on an inside bend where the canyon walls spread two hundred yards apart. It sits at the bottom of the gorge where high cliffs delay the sunrise and bring on an early dusk. A lodge and canteen form the hub of eleven guest cabins, normally booked twenty-two months in advance, four hiker dormitories, and an employee bunkhouse. The oldest cabins, dating to 1922, are those built mainly of stone. The ranch is designed to accommodate ninety-two overnight guests. Rows of cabins face inward as

Canyon Crossroads

A SPUR RIDGE to the east of Phantom Ranch forms a divide between the waters of Bright Angel Creek and the Colorado, which flows full bore down the throat of the Inner Gorge. The deep tones of the river rumble on one side, and the higher-pitched rush of the creek drifts up from the other.

if bracing against the sheer mass of rock lifting above them.

Phantom Ranger Station, together with a weather station and the trail crew bunkhouse, sits on the east side of the creek below the ranch. The Bright Angel Campground, with space for ninety backpackers, begins at the mouth of Bright Angel Canyon and stretches along the west side of the creek, opposite the ranch mule corral. The National Park Service mule corral, helipad, sewage treatment plant, and ranger cabins scatter along the west side of Bright Angel Creek between the delta and Bright Angel Suspension Bridge, also known as the silver bridge. Upriver at the foot of the Kaibab Suspension Bridge lie the Boat Beach, prehistoric ruins, and the grave of Rees Griffiths, a trail crew fore-man killed by rockfall in 1922. Just beyond the bridge is the U.S. Geological Survey gauging station and cableway. Readings are no longer taken by a resident hydro-grapher but are relayed automatically by satellite. This unique community has taken root where the river corridor intersects the transcanyon corridor in the heart of the gorge.

From the ridge above Bright Angel Creek you can watch storms sweep past the North Rim and tumble over the cliffs in cascades of heavy cloud. About eight inches of precipitation reach Phantom each year, only a third of the amount that falls on the Kaibab Plateau a few miles away. But an average year is rare. A scant three inches might fall during one twelve-month period,

A mule deer enjoying the cool waters of Bright Angel Creek.

followed the next year by fourteen inches of rain and a dusting of snow. For those who have only hiked the Grand Canyon in summer, snow at the bottom may come as a surprise. Traces of snow fall most years at Phantom, and on a stormy day in 1939 almost a foot covered the ranch.

Canyon country has two wet seasons. During the summer rainy season, extending from July into September, moist air moves in from the Gulf of Mexico and brings violent thunderstorms. Many of these storms are localized, sometimes packing a third of the year's rainfall into one day while leaving the ground dry only a few miles away. In late fall, Pacific storms begin to dominate the weather patterns. They roll in slowly and take their time leaving, bringing snow to the

Winter visitors look into the inner canyon from above the Bright Angel Trail.

high country and soft, steady rains to the canyons.

Temperatures in winter can drop below freezing at night and then rebound to more than 50°F (10°C) in the afternoon. By summer, daytime temperatures in the canyon normally exceed 100°F (38°C) and have soared to a blistering 120°F (49°C). Milder conditions during the spring and fall draw many hikers into the backcountry. But the weather in those months can swing wildly, at times amassing a season's extremes into a single day. More than once, the midday heat has suddenly given way to cold winds followed by rain and a peppering of hail, coming only a moment before a snow squall blows in. Twenty minutes later you're peeling off layers and watching a patch of blue sky spread overhead.

The Natural World

A Canyon Within a Canyon

BEGINNING AT THE RIM, walls stair-step downward in a succession of cliffs and ledges to give the Grand Canyon its characteristic profile. The cliff-slope-bench pattern keeps repeating until reaching the Inner Gorge where sedimentary layers abruptly give way to older metamorphic and igneous rocks.

These Precambrian rocks project a force barely contained by the orderly laminations above. They form the dark walls of an inner canyon nearly a thousand-feet deep. Almost two billion years old, Vishnu Schist, the dominant formation at Phantom Ranch, began as ocean deposits interlayered with volcanic ash and lava flows. And then its very structure changed. During the collision of crustal plates, slabs were driven downward to great depths, heated and deformed under the tremendous pressure of overlying masses. The veins of red Zoroaster Granite within the dark schist began as magma squeezed into the Vishnu where it slowly cooled.

Other Precambrian formations have eroded away completely from most of the canyon and left a billion-year gap in the geological record, known as The Great Unconformity. But tilted remnants of these younger Precambrian rocks occur in the Phantom Ranch area. The brick-red Hakatai Shale is the most distinctive of these deposits, and the billion-year-old Bass Limestone below it contains fossil algae mats, the earliest evidence of life in the canyon record.

Phantom Ranch lies at the core of the Grand Canyon where the river has

left: The Colorado River cuts through Vishnu Schist, the basement rocks of the Grand Canyon.

cut deeply through the south flank of the Kaibab Plateau. In this section the canyon rims are ten miles apart, with the north side rising a thousand feet higher due to a slight tilt in the bedrock layers. Water on the North Rim drains toward the river following the dip of the rock, but water flows away from the canyon on the South Rim. The underlying geology, combined with more precipitation and a gain in erosional force, has produced tributary canyons twice as long on the North Rim as those across the river. A prime example is Bright Angel Canyon with a fourteen-mile-long trail from the North Rim funneling through it that is twice as long as its counterpart on the south.

Craggy metamorphic rock towers above Phantom Ranch.

Over time the side canyons have gnawed back into both rims, extending the gorge laterally by headward erosion roughly ten times faster than they cut downward. Many factors have contributed to this process: the steady prying of plant roots, an occasional earth tremor, chemical weathering and the freeze-thaw cycle, debris flows and floods, wind, and rain. Most erosion happens slowly, but sometimes the incremental changes build to a dramatic finish. For example, softer shales erode faster than the sandstone and limestone above them, under-cutting the cliffs. When the critical threshold is reached, a massive slab collapses in a tremendous rock-fall. Then a storm unleashes a torrent of rain with rivulets and washes flowing together into ravines, and the ravines emptying into gorges. The flood waters tumble boulders and uproot trees, scouring the canyons with a slurry of debris. Soon the waters subside, and the canyon appears as unchanging as it did before.

Bright Angel Rising

IN DECEMBER 1966 a series of storms hammered the North Rim, unloading an incredible fourteen inches of rain at the entrance station on top of an existing snowpack. Runoff soon began pouring into the gorge below.

The creek rose steadily, and flood-waters churned down Bright Angel Canyon. It swallowed large chunks of the North Kaibab Trail, destroying five of the seven footbridges, and tore out the not yet completed transcanyon pipeline. At Phantom Ranch, which received only two inches of rain, the creek peaked at thirty feet above normal flows and remained at flood levels for three days. It destroyed washrooms, ruined the park service trail crew bunkhouse, and washed away half of the campground. "Trees more than 150 years old," reported the acting park superintendent, "were ripped out like straws."

Another winter storm hit the rim in March 1995, bringing five inches of rain. While less intense than the 1966 event, it was enough. The creek increased more than forty times its normal volume. In the narrows above the ranch, a boulder crashed onto the trail behind a hiker and began rolling. He tried to outrun it and lost the race, receiving a deep gash on his leg.

Floodwaters rumbled past Phantom, shaking the ground. A beaver forgot its fear of humans for the moment and followed them to high ground. Five workers from Phantom Ranch walked down to the mouth of the creek to watch the flood enter the river.

The 1.7 mile River Trail, on the south side the Colorado River, is blasted from the basement rocks of the canyon.

The Colorado River changes color quickly after storms flush sand and debris into it.

storm struck the rim country at the end of summer. Runoff poured into the upper reaches of Phantom Canyon and raced toward the narrows below. A lookout on the rim warned the inner canyon rangers of potential flooding. They ran to the campground and herded everyone to higher ground. Strong winds whipped through camp, followed by the leading edge of a flash flood. Stained a deep red by the rock, the streamflow pushed before it a tangle of fallen trees and other debris.

Earlier in the afternoon, three hikers ventured into Phantom Canyon. Standing next to a waterfall, they didn't hear the approaching flood until it was too late. All they had time to do was duck behind a boulder and face downstream. In an instant, a blast of muddy water jumped over the protecting rock and struck them. Swept off their feet, they were tumbled downstream a short distance into Bright Angel Canyon where only one of the three managed to pull himself to safety. The others, swept past the ranch and into the Colorado River, did not survive.

Boulders washed down by floods form a debris fan at the mouth of the creek. This constricts the river into a

Within fifteen minutes, the creek had jumped behind them and cut off any chance of escape. They found themselves stranded on a low island with the waters rising steadily. Then, as the situation grew desperate, the air temperature dropped. The rain falling high on the rim changed to snow and the creek stopped rising. "I'm totally convinced," said former ranch manager Warren Tracy, "we would have lost them if it hadn't started snowing."

Two years later, an intense thunder-

narrow channel, increasing its velocity and creating Bright Angel Rapid, one of 160 rapids on the Colorado River. Prior to the construction of the Glen Canyon Dam, spring floods would rearrange these debris fans, sweeping the main river channel clear of accumulated rocks and debris. Annual spring floods on the river, cresting at thirty to fifty feet above normal levels, ended in 1963 with the completion of the dam. The new river runs clearer, colder, and more predictable than the old. But it remains a powerful river.

Life at the Bottom

WATER IS THE ONE CONSTANT in the equation for survival. Desert plants, lacking an abundant source, have to survive long dry spells. Leaves tend to be succulent, leathery, or waxy to preserve moisture, while the thick, fleshy pads of the prickly pear cactus store moisture collected even in light rains by its shallow root system. On the other hand, the roots of mesquite trees tap moisture thirty to one hundred feet below the surface. Utah agave and narrow-leaf yucca grow in the drier reaches. At creekside the desert vegetation ends abruptly, replaced by lush riparian growth. A community of water-loving plants, including horsetail and arrowweed, box elder and seep willow, crowds

the bank above a narrow zone scoured by floods.

Canyon animals also have to come to terms with a scarcity of water. Some rodents have found a solution by never drinking. The kangaroo rat can survive on metabolic water obtained from digesting seeds. Mule deer meet much of their water needs by browsing on succulent plants.

Because spring floods no longer scour the banks of the Colorado River, vegetation is allowed to take root in a band below the old high-water line. Native species such as seep willow, coyote willow, and arrowweed have moved in, and honey mesquite and catclaw acacia now grow along the new high-water line.

But non-native species, especially tamarisk, have also taken advantage

The desert prickly pear cactus is common in the Inner Gorge. Its purple fruit is edible.

of the new conditions. More than a century ago, settlers began introducing tamarisk, native to North Africa and Asia, and it now grows throughout the Colorado River drainage. It is one of the most pervasive non-native plants in western North America. Each tree can produce a billion seeds a year, spurring a rapid spread along the river and its tributaries. Tamarisk grows along Bright Angel Creek, but not as densely as it does along some portions of the river.

Phantom Ranch is not only a rare developed canyon oasis, but also a carefully nurtured one. Fruit trees and ornamentals appeared at Phantom almost as soon as people began spending more than a night or two at the bottom of the canyon. Peach, pomegranate, fig, and olive trees now grow in the vicinity, along with a date palm thought to have germinated from a seed casually tossed away by a visitor.

Utah agave can be found from the rim to the river. After 15-25 years this succulent plant flowers, then dies.

Heavy wire mesh holds river rock in place, channeling the creek to keep it within its banks. Fremont cottonwoods are native, but early photos show only a few of them. Trailbuilder David Rust made the first recorded plantings in 1907. From upper Phantom Canyon, he packed four hundred cuttings back to his camp at the mouth of Bright Angel Creek and dug the first irrigation ditches to keep them alive. Rangers continue to replant trees that have died or been washed out by floods. Fencing protects the trees from beavers.

To live in the canyon, wildlife adapts its behavior to the high temperatures. Most animals simply avoid the heat as much as possible. They duck into the shade or burrow below the surface where, on a 100°F (38°C) day, the temperature a foot underground is only half of what it is above. In extreme heat, the pocket mouse slips into a state of estivation, similar to hibernation, where the body temperature drops and activity slows dramatically. Reptiles, being cold-blooded creatures, are sensitive to ambient temperatures. Lizards need to dart into the shade frequently, and snakes can stand only a few minutes of exposure to the midday sun.

As the heat of day lessens and the shadows grow, Bright Angel Canyon comes alive. First the lizards appear, feeding on insects, and birds begin to forage. The air cools, and ground squirrels start investigating their territory. Burrowing animals emerge at dusk, along with bats. Flowering plants open to attract the moths and bats needed for pollination. Night is also when scorpions become active. The bark scorpion, pale yellow and about two inches long, is found under rocks and in the shaggy bark of cottonwoods. Drop for drop, its venom is more poisonous than rattlesnake venom but rarely fatal.

Claretcup hedgehog cactus grows in large mounds. When in bloom, its flowers are a deep red.

For years the ringtail, a relative of the raccoon, marauded at night through the campground. A flashlight might find one darting by with its banded tail held high or catch the light reflecting from its large, night-adapted eyes. But food boxes at each campsite have reduced the number of encounters and have helped to prevent foraging mule deer from consuming human food and packaging.

Each cottonwood tree along the creek helps moderate the desert conditions by transpiring fifty gallons of moisture a day. John Hance, an early canyon guide, learned about transpiration when he led a sightseeing party down the trail. As they descended, a young woman gave him a botany lesson on how trees breathe. The old guide mulled over this new information. "That explains something that has puzzled me a long time," he said. "I used to make camp under a big mesquite tree, and night after night that thing would keep me awake with its snoring."

A Phantom Past

BELOW THE KAIBAB SUSPENSION Bridge lie the remains of an ancient pueblo. Brittlebush and a few acacias are scattered over the ancestral Puebloan site whose beginnings trace back to A.D. 1050, during a time of increased precipitation and growing populations.

The L-shaped roomblock faces southeast, a good direction to catch the winter sun. It contains four small rooms for sleeping, a storage room, and a detached kiva used as a ceremonial chamber. As many as sixteen people may have lived here, growing the staple crops of corn, beans, and squash. Their efforts to farm these marginal lands were supplemented by gathering wild plants and hunting. Probably an outlier of a large settlement on the rim, the pueblo grew in stages over the course of two periods of occupation until its final abandonment in 1140. Toward the end, inhabitants were trading less with outsiders, indicating a time of growing isolation as people throughout the canyon began to leave.

Douglas Schwartz, of the American School of Research, excavated the site in 1969. "These ancient people, who time and again moved into the canyon country," he wrote, "lived on the edge of splendor and desperation."

Ancestors of the Havasupai, Hualapai, and Paiute entered the region from the west about two centuries before the first Europeans arrived. The Havasupai continue to live in Havasu Canyon, a major branch of the Grand Canyon. Other American Indians have

left: Prehistoric Puebloan kiva and room blocks near Phantom Ranch.

traditions connecting them to this region. Certain Zuni clans claim a location within Bright Angel Canyon as their place of origin where people first entered this world. The Hopi occasionally return to visit shrines and have undertaken pilgrimages to gather salt along the river. The Navajo also used these deposits, and in the 1860s they took refuge in the canyon.

Havasupai kohot or chief.

On his first river expedition in 1869, John Wesley Powell allowed his men a layover day at the mouth of Bright Angel Creek. The river had taken its toll on them, and the expedition had turned into a struggle for survival. For weeks they had faced constant danger and the daily grind of lining boats through rapids and portaging heavy gear. Food was running low, and they were reduced to a diet of moldy flour, some dried fruit, and plenty of coffee. Searching up the creek, they found a large pine log and cut three oars from it to replace those they had lost. "The cook," noted expedition member George Bradley, "having spread all the rations to dry, was engaged making oars when the boat swung around by the eddy tide; the rope caught the box of soda and drew it all into the river so we

must eat 'unleavened bread' all the rest of the trip."

For the next quarter century, recorded visits to Bright Angel Creek were rare. Robert Stanton, surveying the river in 1890, reached the creek and found it an "enchanting spot." By then, prospectors had begun probing the inner canyon and occasionally staking claims. Dan Hogan, a miner and later a Rough Rider during the Spanish-American War, swam the river in 1890 to prospect in Bright Angel Canyon. The next year he investigated the upper end of the gorge, trapping beaver along the way, as he completed the first known cross-canyon trip through the main corridor.

"Conditions at the Grand Canyon were a bit raw in 1902," wrote François Matthes of the U.S. Geological Survey. That year he began the challenging job of mapping this "chasm of labyrinthine intricacy." Hearing that Bright Angel Canyon could not be traversed by pack animals and might be impassable to a man on foot, he crossed downriver at the foot of the Bass Trail. The survey party worked back along the North Rim until reaching the head of Bright Angel Canyon in the fall. They began searching for a route into the gorge as the weather threatened when they

*François Matthes mapping
the Grand Canyon, 1904.*

encountered "two haggard men and a weary burro" emerging from below. Sidney Ferrell and Jim Murray, who had been trapping and prospecting, described their route up Bright Angel Canyon to Matthes, who sent two men ahead to clear a rough path. The party of four surveyors descended with their pack train of horses and mules.

"So steep was it in certain places," wrote Matthes, "that the animals fairly slid down on their haunches." After reaching the canyon floor, they crossed the creek ninety-four times and took several days to map its course. At the river they borrowed a boat from a prospector. Their animals eagerly swam across, sensing they were homeward bound. The following year Matthes packed in a steel boat by mule and began using the trail as his regular access route into the central canyon. After thirty-six months of fieldwork, he completed the first detailed map of the Grand Canyon.

When Matthes returned in 1903 for a second season, David Rust already had a crew improving his route down Bright Angel Canyon. Rust, a Stanford-educated schoolteacher turned trail foreman, was building a trail from the North Rim to the river where he planned to string a cableway to connect with trails on the south side. During his trail work, Rust kept a journal and on July 29, 1906, entered: "Rest and

Cooking at Rust's Camp.

laundry. Read the papers. One burro goes over ledge with pack, burro dies."

After completing the trail, his crew brought down the cable. They reached the river on October 4, 1906, and met a party led by Sid Ferrell, who had pointed Matthes in the right direction four years before. Two of Ferrell's burros had drowned in the crossing,

Photographer Emery Kolb with wife Blanche and daughter Edith on Rust's cableway.

so Rust loaned him a couple of horses to continue on to the North Rim. Ferrell's wife accompanied him, and she became the first woman to make the rim-to-rim crossing. Rust struggled for months to rig the cable with a car large enough to carry one mule. Even a bout of pneumonia didn't stop him. Finally on September 22, 1907, he

made a terse entry. "No use to say more—the tram runs O.K. and looks pretty good."

During work on the trail, Rust had established a camp near where Phantom Ranch now stands. Hunting parties and sightseers began to stay overnight at "Rust's Camp." He planted fruit and shade trees, irrigated by the creek, set up tents for his guests, and built a ramada for shade. Teddy Roosevelt used the cableway in 1913 on his way to hunt mountain lions on the North Rim. After he spent a night at the bottom, the name changed to "Roosevelt's Camp."

Colter's Dream

GRAND CANYON BECAME a national park in 1919, and two years later a wooden suspension bridge replaced Rust's cable car, allowing mule riders to reach the north side of the canyon with relative ease. As the Inner Gorge became more accessible to visitors, a need grew for overnight accommodations at the bottom of the canyon. Mary Elizabeth Jane Colter, architect for the Santa Fe Railroad, drew up the plans for a lodge on Bright Angel Creek based on the western ranches she had visited. In a period when architects often found their inspiration in European works, Colter designed buildings that drew upon the region's cultural traditions. She borrowed what worked aesthetically from Spanish influences, Pueblo Indians, even miners and cattlemen.

Instead of trying to compete with the dramatic landscape, she incorporated local materials to blend with it. The cabins were wood-frame structures with walls of uncut boulders, reflecting the Craftsman Bungalow style popular at the time. Colter intentionally softened the lines of some buildings by having the wide stone corners taper upward. Massive rocks set into the foundations tie the cabins visually to the canyon floor. She had the exterior trim and doors painted in dark blue, green, and deep yellow. Furnishings inside the cabins were kept simple but comfortable: a desk and chair, a couple of beds covered with bedspreads depicting a Hopi sunshield or thunderbird, and a Navajo rug spread on the tile floor. Each building had its own character, and she set them apart at irregular intervals to break up any sense of regimentation.

Mary Colter

Activity on a working ranch revolved around a main house surrounded by a bunkhouse, barn, corrals, a couple of sheds, and maybe a blacksmith shop. Colter's design for Phantom Ranch placed the dining

The stone-and-wood cabins at Phantom Ranch have changed little since the 1920s.

Recreation hall and pool, 1930s.

room/kitchen at the center with the guest cabins clustering around it. The original plan called for only five buildings at a cost of $20,000, and all construction materials except the stone had to be hauled down by mule. The canyon resort opened in 1922 and quickly expanded to meet the growing demand. Colter added tents and additional cabins, a recreation hall and bathhouse, and increased the dining area. Major construction ended in 1930, and the basic layout of the ranch has changed little since then.

Phantom Ranch became a fashionable getaway in the 1920s for socialites and celebrities wanting to rough it in comfort. While never a working ranch, it did try to be as self-sufficient as possible. Ranch hands expanded an existing orchard and planted a garden, grew alfalfa, and raised chickens and rabbits for Sunday dinners. For breakfast they offered local eggs and homemade nectarine jam. The ranch had a primitive telephone service from the

Packing a washing machine to Phantom Ranch, circa 1939.

start, and a generator installed in 1926 produced electricity for the ranch. But once a week the packer had to haul down a load of coal for the kitchen range.

During a career spanning forty-six years, Colter continued to design buildings and oversee their construction for the Fred Harvey Company. Her unique style can be found in other structures at the Grand Canyon: Hermits Rest, Bright Angel Lodge, Lookout Studio, Hopi House, and the Watchtower at Desert View. "There was only one Mary Jane Colter," said Mike Harrison, who worked for the park service in the 1920s. "She was a woman among men. Everybody liked her. She knew what she was about."

Trailbuilders

DAVID RUST'S TRAMWAY was replaced by a suspension bridge a year before Phantom Ranch opened. During construction, three pack horses, carrying loads that included more than one-hundred pounds of TNT, slipped over a cliff and were killed on the rocks below. When the bridge was completed, high winds tossed it about so violently no one could cross, and several times it flipped completely over. "The bridge we used," wrote early visitor Francis Line, "seemed as slender and fragile as

a fishing rod, swaying in the wind without a person on it."

In 1928 the National Park Service borrowed an experienced U.S. Forest Service crew to oversee construction of a more stable bridge. The heat caused a 300 percent turnover in the work force, despite running a night shift using floodlights. To bring in the main bridge cables, a crew of forty-two men was hired, mostly Havasupai Indians accustomed to the heat. They spaced themselves along the length of the cable, which weighed more than a ton, hoisted it onto their shoulders, and snaked their way down the South Kaibab Trail.

Mule train hauling building materials for construction of the Kaibab Suspension Bridge, 1928.

Between trips, the Havasupai prepared for the next round by taking sweat baths in a large, tunnel-shaped lodge built on the bank of the river. The finished bridge stood 440-feet long, 5-feet wide, and 65-feet above the river. It required that ninety-four tons of material be hauled down the trail, but no man or pack animal was seriously injured during its construction.

Running cable for the Kaibab Suspension Bridge was a death-defying act.

In the 1930s Company 818 of the Civilian Conservation Corps established a winter camp at the mouth of Bright Angel Canyon. The two hundred young men built footbridges, a mule corral and cabin for the park service, and a camp for themselves, which evolved into the Bright Angel Campground. They replaced the original transcanyon telephone line with one less prone to

breakdowns and dug a swimming pool at Phantom Ranch, which they shared with the lodge guests. Difficult to maintain, the pool was filled in during the winter of 1972. But much of the CCC's efforts were focused on improving the inner-canyon trail system. They built the Clear Creek Trail, connecting Phantom Ranch with a perennial stream nine miles to the east, and by 1936 had linked the Bright Angel Trail with the South Kaibab. Men suspended from 150-foot ropes cut sections of the 1.7-mile-long River Trail with jack-hammers, and others blasted a route across sheer cliffs, using 40,000 pounds of gunpowder in the process.

In their off-hours the CCC boys spent time in the recreation hall with its library, canteen, and game room. When the opportunity came to add a pool table, half the camp volunteered to retrieve it from the rim. Within a day and a half they had hauled the slate slabs and other pieces down the trail and reassembled them in the recreation hall.

At Phantom Ranch, an early ranch manager found another way of entertaining himself. Night after night, he joined poker games with the mule wranglers. He not only kept losing his money but also ignored his wife's advice to stop. Finally she got his attention by pulling out a six-shooter and firing into the ceiling to break up the game.

Mule riders cling to the cliff walls on a narrow corridor trail.

Visitors entered the canyon in droves during the construction boom of the 1920s and 1930s. Trail guide Art Metzger, who led his first party when he was only ten years old, said they carried smelling salts in those days to revive riders when they grew faint at places like the Devils Corkscrew. On one outing, a party of schoolteachers kept hammering a guide with questions about the canyon. By the time they came in sight of a rock cairn and wanted to know its significance, he was played out. "Well," he said, "a guide one time had a bunch of schoolteachers down here and they talked the leg off him. So they just buried him there and put up a monument."

Park naturalist Edwin McKee found the new cross-canyon trail particularly useful in 1929. On weekends he would hike across to the North Rim to visit his girlfriend, Barbara Hastings, until the day came when she met him halfway, at Phantom Ranch, and he proposed. Eddie became a legendary geologist, and in 1964 accompanied a party of fourteen astronauts on a field session down the South Kaibab Trail. After spending the night at Phantom Ranch, they hiked up to Indian Garden where they mounted mules for the remainder of the trip.

Each year about 10,000 riders enter the canyon, and backpackers spend nearly 50,000 nights camped in the central corridor. The National Park Service completed the South Kaibab Trail in 1925 and later made extensive improvements to the old Bright Angel Trail. They also rerouted the upper end of the North Kaibab Trail, normally open from late spring through mid-autumn. These corridor trails are officially included in the National Trails System.

Trail's End

AN EARLY SANTA FE RAILWAY brochure described Phantom Ranch as being wrapped in "an atmosphere of unreality, thousands of feet down in the heart of the earth." Mary Colter chose a style of architecture that heightened this sense of a place lost in time. That is part of its appeal. But a sophisticated technology supports it, lying just below the surface or tucked out of sight.

Electricity comes from a buried line, linking the ranch to the outside power grid, and a microwave dish provides telephone service. Each summer day the ranch uses 7,000 gallons of water and the campground another 3,000. The water comes from Roaring Springs near the head of Bright Angel Canyon where it is filtered and treated before being piped downcanyon. The trans-canyon pipeline continues to the South Rim, supplying Grand Canyon Village with 500,000 gallons of water a day.

Even the exterior of the sewage treatment plant at Bright Angel Creek fits the rough-hewn image of the place. But inside the operations center a series of computers monitors the treatment process and links the plant to a park-wide network. Pack strings still haul out the trash and bring in supplies, including two-and-a-half tons of food each week and occasionally special requests like a Christmas tree. In addition, the ranch runs an elaborate composting system, which handles up to eighty pounds of garbage a day.

The daily routine at Phantom Ranch starts early. By 2:00 a.m. the

left: The canteen serves as front desk, restaurant, bar, gift shop, and recreation hall.

breakfast cook is in the kitchen and the day begins. The morning waiter arrives at 4:30 and serves an early breakfast half an hour later. The breakfast bell rings at 6:30, but sunlight won't reach the canyon floor until mid-morning. Like stagehands changing sets, the Phantom crew transforms the dining hall into a canteen at 8:00, back to a restaurant for dinner, and then to a beer hall for a couple of hours in the evening. The last shift converts every-thing back to a restaurant, sets up for breakfast, and turns the lights off at 11:00 p.m. During the day, other workers are cleaning rooms, washing and folding sheets, doing maintenance. It takes a staff of seventeen, with each person working several different jobs, to keep the ranch running smoothly.

Phantom Ranch employees work for ten days straight before getting four off. To go "upstairs" to the rim, they walk. But some residents prefer to stay. Originally from the Netherlands, National Park Sevice volunteer Sjors Horstman has lived at Phantom for many years and rarely leaves. He spends much of his summers handling heat-related emergencies and advising hikers on how to climb out of the hole they got themselves into. He also replants native cottonwoods, velvet ash, and box elder in trampled areas need-ing revegetation or where floods have ripped out the old trees. On the sunny side of the corral he has planted a row of shade trees for the mules. He has found his niche. "Whenever I get out," he said, "I can't wait to get back."

Long tables inside the canteen accommodate family-style meals and evening card games.

Before becoming a National Park Service ranger, Pam Cox decided to challenge herself by hiking into the Grand Canyon. The four days she spent at the bottom worked their magic on her. "It literally changed my life," she said. "I decided to find some way of coming back as a ranger at Phantom." She worked as a seasonal ranger at Mount Rainier National Park until completing a degree in geology, and in 1997 she returned to Phantom as an inner-canyon ranger. "It's a dream come true," she said.

Rangers assigned to Phantom Ranch spend nine days working in the canyon and five days on the rim during their time off. A typical workday for Pam begins at 7:00 in the morning and doesn't end until 9:00 at night. Each day she leads a nature walk and gives two interpretive programs, posts the daily weather report, assists the law-enforcement ranger, handles medical emergencies, and tries to foster a sense of stewardship for Grand Canyon among visitors. She once spent three hours counseling a family afraid to hike out, encouraging them and providing tips on how to safely undertake the return trip. "Sometimes," Pam said, "people have to reach within themselves and find a strength they didn't realize was there."

People return to Phantom Ranch, year after year, to regain a certain perspective. Part of it comes from the sense of remoteness and part comes from the sheer massive scale of the surroundings. The canyon also works its magic on those who live within it.

Phantom Ranch cabins blend with the natural surroundings while providing rustic comfort for travelers.

Warren and Elaine Tracy worked at Phantom for a dozen years. On January 1, 2000, they rented the entire ranch, combining their savings with current and former employee's so they could celebrate the new millennium together. "When you live here," Warren said, "your priorities become clearer. You learn what's important in life—it's people. All we're left with is each other."

And sometimes a few critters. Stories have circulated around Phantom for years about a wild turkey nicknamed Kathy. Blown in by a storm from the North Rim, the turkey boldly criss-crossed the inner canyon for more than a decade before a bobcat pounced on her at Indian Garden. She would often hang out at the Bright Angel Campground, perched in a tree, or join a line of hikers on the trail, stopping when they stopped and joining them again when they continued. The wild turkey once got all the mules dancing frantically on the suspension bridge when she marched right through a pack string.

Warren remembered his first Thanksgiving at Phantom when Kathy flew up to the dining hall window after everyone had sat down. "She kept staring in as we ate," he said. "And yes, it was a turkey dinner."

Visiting Phantom Ranch

TODAY PHANTOM RANCH REMAINS accessible only by foot, mule, or raft. To stay at the ranch reservations are required and must be made well in advance through the park's concessioner. Snacks are available at the canteen, but meals are by reservation only. The concessioner also manages the popular mule rides into the canyon. Phantom Ranch is accessible by mule from the South Rim only. Overnight stays at Bright Angel Campground, located a short distance from the ranch along Bright Angel Creek, require a permit issued through the National Park Service backcountry office. Most hikers and all mule riders to Phantom Ranch spend at least one night at the bottom.

And what do some folks find to be the most unique thing about Phantom Ranch? Well, for the cost of regular postage, they can mail a postcard or letter—by mule—from the bottom of the Grand Canyon.

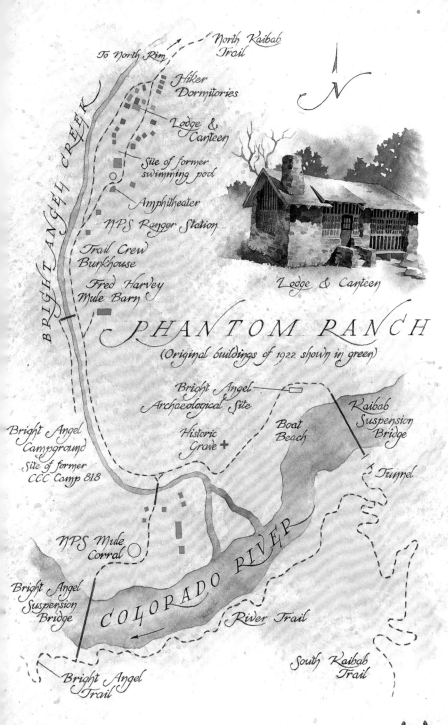

North Kaibab
Trail

To North Rim

Hiker
Dormitories

Lodge &
Canteen

Site of former
swimming pool

Amphitheater

NPS Ranger Station

Trail Crew
Bunkhouse

Fred Harvey
Mule Barn

BRIGHT ANGEL CREEK

Lodge & Canteen

PHANTOM RANCH

(Original buildings of 1922 shown in green)

Bright Angel
Archaeological Site

Bright Angel
Campground

Site of former
CCC Camp 818

Historic
Grave ✝

Boat
Beach

Kaibab
Suspension
Bridge

Tunnel

NPS Mule
Corral

COLORADO RIVER

Bright Angel
Suspension
Bridge

River Trail

Bright Angel
Trail

South Kaibab
Trail

Suggested Reading

Michael Anderson, *Living at the Edge: Explorers, Exploiters and Settlers of the Grand Canyon Region*, 1998, Grand Canyon Association.

Grand Canyon Mule Ride Video, 40 minutes,
Don Briggs Productions.

Virginia L. Grattan, *Mary Colter: Builder Upon the Red Earth*,
1992, Grand Canyon Natural History Association.

Rose Houk, *An Introduction to Grand Canyon Ecology*,
1996, Grand Canyon Association.

Allyson Mathis, *Grand Canyon Yardstick of Geologic Time*,
2006, Grand Canyon Association.

L. Greer Price, *An Introduction to Grand Canyon Geology*,
1999, Grand Canyon Association.

Karen L. Taylor, *Grand Canyon's Long-Eared Taxi*,
1992, Grand Canyon Natural History Association.

Scott Thybony, *Official Guide to Hiking the Grand Canyon*,
2005 Revision, Grand Canyon Association.

Stephen R. Whitney, *A Field Guide to the Grand Canyon*,
1996, The Mountaineers.